Our Resources

William B. Rice

Consultant

Catherine Hollinger, CID, CLIA
EPA WaterSense Partner
Environmental Consultant

Publishing Credits

Rachelle Cracchiolo, M.S.Ed., *Publisher*
Conni Medina, M.A.Ed., *Managing Editor*
Diana Kenney, M.A.Ed., NBCT, *Senior Editor*
Dona Herweck Rice, *Series Developer*
Robin Erickson, *Multimedia Designer*
Timothy Bradley, *Illustrator*

Image Credits: Cover, p.1 arquiplay77/iStock; p.19
Courtney Patterson; pp.28, 29 J.J.Rudisill; p.25 MCT/
Newscom; p.8 The Granger Collection, New York; p.22,
23 Travis Hanson; p.13 Wikimedia Commons; p.13 Wild
Wonders of Europe / Lundgren / naturepl.com; all other
images from Shutterstock.

Library of Congress Cataloging-in-Publication Data

Rice, William B. (William Benjamin), 1961- author.
  Our resources / William B. Rice.
    pages cm
  Summary: "Almost everything you do requires
resources. You use them throughout your day. Our planet
provides us with natural resources, such as water, wood,
oil, and metal. Whether resources are renewable or
nonrenewable, they provide us with important materials
we need."-- Provided by publisher.
  Audience: Grades 4 to 6.
  Includes index.
  ISBN 978-1-4807-4689-3 (pbk.)
  1. Natural resources--Juvenile literature. I. Title.
HC85.R5327 2016
333.7--dc23
                                        2014045212

Teacher Created Materials

5301 Oceanus Drive
Huntington Beach, CA 92649-1030
http://www.tcmpub.com

ISBN 978-1-4807-4689-3

© 2016 Teacher Created Materials, Inc.

Table of Contents

A Day in the Life

Alonzo woke to a buzzing alarm clock. "Shhh!" he mumbled as he rolled out from under the covers. He shuffled to the bathroom and turned on the shower to warm up the water. He brushed his teeth while he waited. Then, it was time to soap up and shampoo. Finally, he felt awake!

Alonzo pulled some jeans, rubber-soled sneakers, and a cotton shirt from his closet. Dressed and ready, he went to the kitchen and got milk and juice from the fridge. He poured cereal from a box, added milk, and ate his breakfast while he read about last night's game on his smartphone. Then, putting his cup and bowl in the dishwasher, he grabbed his bag and headed out the door. He jumped in his car and drove to school just in time for computer lab.

Alonzo went from class to class, ate a hot lunch with his friends, and finished the day with swimming practice in the school's solar-heated pool. Then, he drove home, where he flipped on his laptop, did some homework, and read a book on his tablet until dinner. He cooked kabobs on the grill with his family, and then they played video games until bedtime.

Good night!

Now, here's the question. How many resources does Alonzo need to get through his day? The answer is: more than we can count!

What Are Resources?

A resource is a material, a good, or an asset that offers a benefit. The benefit may be to satisfy a need or a want. It may be to provide wealth, enhance well-being, or help a system run smoothly.

If you need or want something, a resource will take care of it. Are you thirsty? Drink a glass of water. The water and the cup are resources. Are you cold? Put on a jacket or turn on the heater. The jacket and heater as well as the gas that runs the heater are resources, too.

Each day, we use many different things in different ways. We use water for drinking, taking showers, and cleaning clothes. We use clothes to stay warm and protect our bodies. We use cars, buses, trains, and planes for transportation. We use telephones and televisions, computers and DVD players. We live in houses, shop in stores, and eat in restaurants. All these things are resources.

Materials

All resources are made from one or more materials. Think of a car. It has hundreds of parts made of glass, plastic, fiber, rubber, and metals. It runs on gasoline, water, and motor oil. All these materials are resources, too.

Three Important Things

Every resource has three important characteristics: *utility* (its ability to satisfy a need or want), *availability* (how much there is), and *potential* (the possibility that it will get used up).

potential

availability

utility

Freshwater is a resource we all need to live. The total amount of freshwater on Earth if it were rolled into a giant ball would be nearly 56 kilometers (34.8 miles) in diameter!

Humans Need Resources

Every person on the planet needs resources to live. Even the most basic lifestyle still needs resources. People need water to drink. We need food to eat. We need clothing to stay warm. We need shelter for protection. We need air to breathe, too. These resources are needed just to stay alive.

More **complex** societies use more resources. The amount of resources that a society can access and use determines how complex the society can be. In early days, people spent their time gathering and hunting food just to stay alive. As they developed easier ways to find, grow, and make food, they had more time available to get and use more resources. These societies developed and grew because they had more resources to use.

European Exploration

From about 1500 to 1800, European explorers traveled the world in a great age of exploration. Their main mission was to trade and find resources.

People began to travel the world, exploring and collecting resources. Often, they tried to use those resources to advance society. Unfortunately, sometimes they took what wasn't theirs to take.

Spices are resources that were sought by early explorers.

Biological Value

Living things need resources with **biological** value. That means the resource fulfills a basic need of the living things, such as food or water.

Natural Resources

Among the many resources in the world, most are made by Mother Earth. These are **natural resources**. People use them to make useful products. We can think of these products as resources, too. A natural resource is something that comes from nature. Some natural resources are found all over Earth. Sunlight and air are two such resources. We are in no danger of losing these resources. Some resources are found in some places but not everywhere. Some areas have much more of a resource than other areas do. In fact, it may be **scarce** in some areas. Resources such as freshwater, iron ore, and **fossil fuels** are like that.

Top Five

Here are the five most used natural resources in the world:

- water
- oil
- natural gas
- phosphorus
- coal

In 1816, natural gas was first used to light a street in Baltimore.

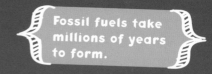
Fossil fuels take millions of years to form.

Some resources are taken from living or once-living material. They include things such as trees, animals, and crops. Mineral resources include ores of heavy metals such as iron, copper, and gold. Fossil fuel resources include crude oil, natural gas, and coal.

livestock

gold

coal

Renewable Resources

Some natural resources are **renewable**. They can be replenished or refilled. They can last forever if they are managed well. But if they are overused, they won't have enough time to replenish. A renewable resource is like the money a person earns for a job. He or she only earns so much every paycheck. Spending more than is earned puts the person in danger of not having enough. Overuse of resources puts those items in danger, too.

Renewable resources renew at a set rate. They can't go faster. If they are used up quicker than they replenish, they won't be renewed fast enough for human use. For instance, soil takes up to thousands of years to become healthy enough for plants to grow. Once it is overused, it may take that many years to become healthy again.

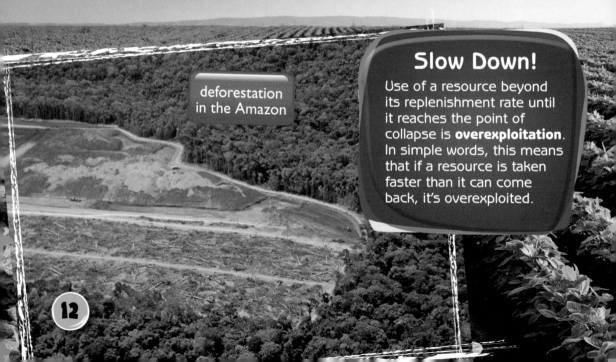

deforestation in the Amazon

Slow Down!

Use of a resource beyond its replenishment rate until it reaches the point of collapse is **overexploitation**. In simple words, this means that if a resource is taken faster than it can come back, it's overexploited.

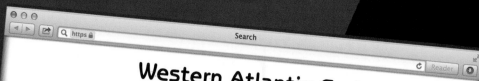

Western Atlantic Cod

For centuries, the Western Atlantic Cod was a popular food. It was fished in large amounts. By the 1970s, it had been fished beyond its ability to replenish. The population collapsed and has not recovered. The loss of large numbers of the cod has also severely affected its ecosystem.

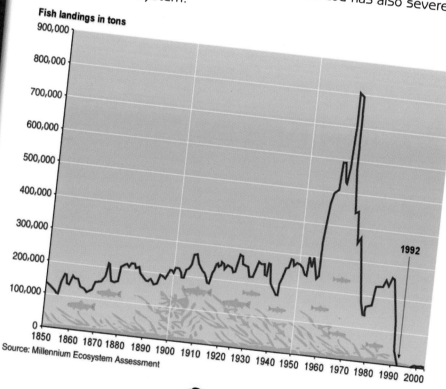

Fish landings in tons

1992

Source: Millennium Ecosystem Assessment

Forests

Forests are renewable because they're made of plants. New plants are always growing in forests. Trees and other plants are there in large quantities. The most important resource that forests provide is wood. We use wood from trees in many different ways. Most houses are built using wood. Chairs, cabinets, and tables are often built with wood. Many musical instruments are built with wood, too. And wood not only provides warmth in fireplaces, it also provides warmth with its beauty.

Forests are important parts of many ecosystems. They provide food and homes to many animals. They also help fill the air with the oxygen we need to breathe.

Where would we all be without this tremendous resource?

light energy

oxygen

carbon dioxide

Cities need forests to keep them cool. Buildings and pavement trap and store heat, but trees help to lower the temperature.

Inhale...Exhale...

The trees and plants that fill forests play an important role in the oxygen cycle. Plants use photosynthesis to take carbon dioxide out of the air and turn it into oxygen. People need oxygen to breathe. Thank you, trees!

This forest is healthy.

This forest is barren.

Water

Water is one of the most important resources on Earth. It's a unique and wonderful substance. Without water, there would be no life on our planet. We need it to live. We need it to help grow the food we eat, and we need it for our bodies to be healthy.

But, we have found many other uses, too. We use it for swimming, boating, and surfing. We use it for water fights and balloon-toss games. We use it to clean clothes and dishes. It helps to cool buildings and factories. It helps us manufacture machines.

Water vapor fills our atmosphere and is the primary element of Earth's climate. Our oceans are enormous pools of water that are home to thousands of plants and animals. Our lakes, rivers, streams, and groundwater are replenished with water from rain and snow.

Human Resources

One of the main reasons humans have been able to live successfully in many environments is that we're social animals. We are resources for one another. We thrive because we live and work together. We survive because we help one another.

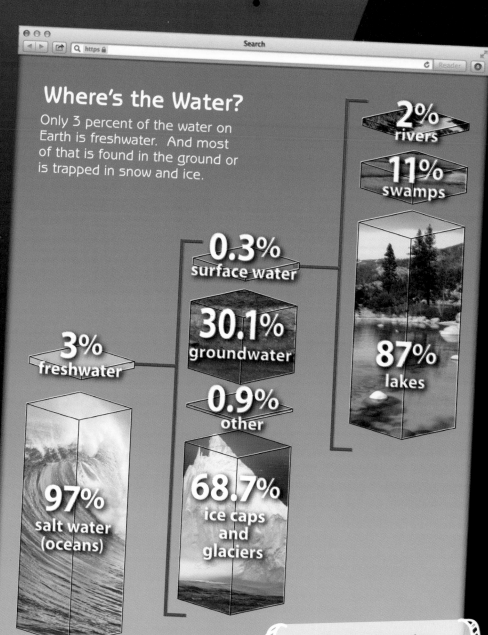

Where's the Water?

Only 3 percent of the water on Earth is freshwater. And most of that is found in the ground or is trapped in snow and ice.

2% rivers

11% swamps

0.3% surface water

30.1% groundwater

87% lakes

3% freshwater

0.9% other

97% salt water (oceans)

68.7% ice caps and glaciers

Groundwater is under Earth's surface and may sit for thousands of years before being used.

Nonrenewable Resources

Nonrenewable resources can be used only once. After that, it may take millions of years for Earth to re-create them, if ever. It's like winning the lottery, in which there's a big amount—but you only get that amount once. When it's gone, it's gone.

electric car charging station

Stop and Think

Since gasoline is a nonrenewable resource, people are trying to find new ways to fuel cars. Vegetable oil is one fuel people have discovered. There are also electric cars that have reduced and even eliminated the need for gasoline in some vehicles. What will you think of?

Fossil Fuels

In most countries, fossil fuels are a crucial energy resource. Fossil fuels are substances such as crude oil, coal, and natural gas. They provide energy to power almost all our **industries**. Crude oil is used to make gasoline, diesel fuel, and jet fuel. Coal and natural gas are used to make electricity. Just think what would happen if we didn't have these resources!

We get fossil fuels from under Earth's surface. Earth has a lot of these resources but not an endless supply. Once we use them up, that's it. It takes Earth millions of years to make more.

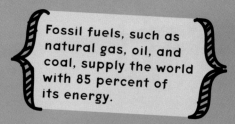

How Much Is Left?

These are the estimated years we have left of fossil fuels on Earth.

Years Left

200
180
160
140
120
100
80
60
40
20

coal   oil   natural gas

Fossil Fuels

Metal Ores

Many of the things we use every day have metal parts. Metals are a resource we use often. We get metals from under Earth's surface from rocks called *ores*.

Ores are a nonrenewable resource. There are plenty of ores. But there aren't always enough to make it worth getting the metal out. It may take more energy and money to get the metal than the metal is worth.

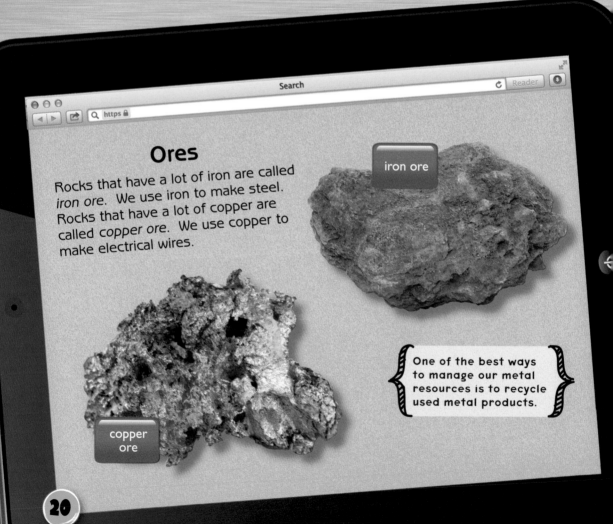

Ores

Rocks that have a lot of iron are called *iron ore*. We use iron to make steel. Rocks that have a lot of copper are called *copper ore*. We use copper to make electrical wires.

iron ore

copper ore

One of the best ways to manage our metal resources is to recycle used metal products.

Radioactive Fuels

We use **radioactive** fuels to make electricity. These are special metals from below Earth's surface. They give off energy when they are broken down. Uranium is a radioactive metal. It puts out a lot of heat. We can use it to make electricity. Some radioactive metals can be dangerous. And they can last for millions of years.

There isn't much uranium ore on Earth. And there isn't much uranium in uranium ore! We have to use a lot of fossil fuels to get the metal from the ore. Someday, it won't be worth getting the uranium out of the ground.

The international symbol for radiation is used to warn people to protect themselves from radioactive materials.

Seven grams of uranium can do the same work as 3.5 barrels of oil or 1,779 pounds of coal.

Finding, Getting, and Using Resources

Many resources are easy to see or find. But some resources are underground. There are many steps in the process of finding them. First, a scientist or engineer walks over an area and looks at and tests the rocks. If things look promising, he or she studies them even more closely. That may involve drilling holes in the ground to look below the surface. The scientist or engineer observes and measures. That information is used to help decide whether to take a resource from the ground. Mining coal and pumping crude oil is done in this way. It is called **extraction**.

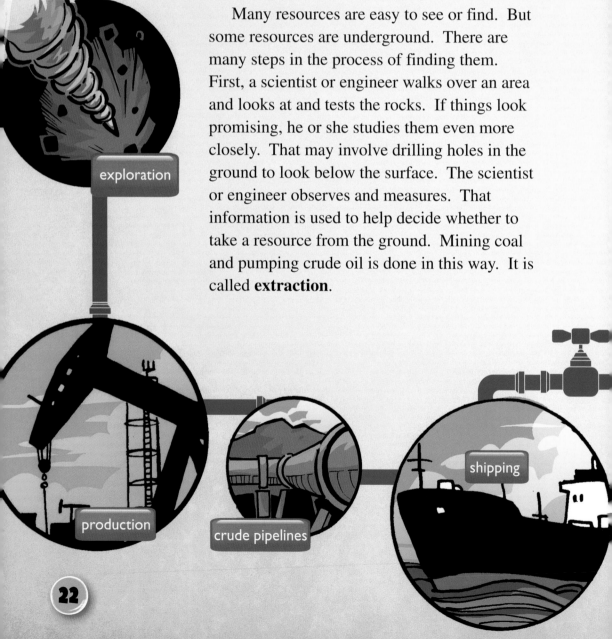

exploration

production

crude pipelines

shipping

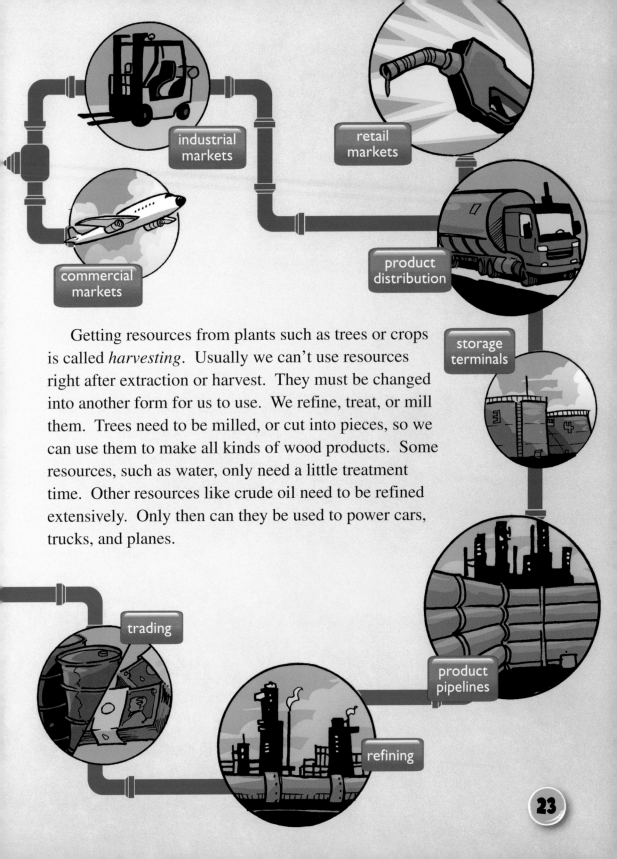

industrial
markets

retail
markets

commercial
markets

product
distribution

storage
terminals

Getting resources from plants such as trees or crops is called *harvesting*. Usually we can't use resources right after extraction or harvest. They must be changed into another form for us to use. We refine, treat, or mill them. Trees need to be milled, or cut into pieces, so we can use them to make all kinds of wood products. Some resources, such as water, only need a little treatment time. Other resources like crude oil need to be refined extensively. Only then can they be used to power cars, trucks, and planes.

trading

product
pipelines

refining

The Human Factor

The world is rich with resources. But resources have their limits. They can be **depleted** if we are reckless with them. They can be damaged if we don't use them wisely. Poor management on our part can have bad results for us. The environment can suffer.

Pollution is a major threat to our resources. We pollute our air, water, and land with **chemicals** and trash. Overusing one resource can pollute another one.

Ogallala aquifer

The Ogallala Aquifer

The Ogallala (o-guy-AL-a) **aquifer** in the Great Plains of the United States was filled up thousands of years ago by glacial meltwater. It has a low replenishment rate, but it has been heavily used. It may take 10,000 to 100,000 years to replenish many parts of the aquifer!

Depletion is another threat. It comes from bad resource management. It happens when we use a resource faster than it can be replenished. The available amount of the resource is reduced in a big way. If we continue to deplete the resource, we risk running out. When a resource is overexploited, it can cause dangerous effects that last for hundreds of years.

Trash Trap

The Great Pacific Garbage Patch is a huge ocean area that traps nondegradable trash from North America and Asia. It's about 19 million square kilometers (7 million square miles) in size!

Trash at Sea

Pacific Ocean

JAPAN

U.S.

1. Trash enters sea from land.

2. Trash is caught by the currents.

3. Trash carpet is formed. Surface water contains six times more plastic than plankton.

Hawaii, U.S.

© 2006 MCT
Source: Greenpeace
Graphic: Jutta Scheibe,
Morten Lyhne

The world is rich with resources. It offers everything that Alonzo, you, and I need to live well. The planet also has an amazing way of restoring itself. Our challenge as human beings is to make good use of the resources while we also protect them for the future. What we do now affects our children and their children. It's our job to be sure they have what they need to survive and thrive, just as we do.

The important thing to remember is this: Earth will survive and heal even if we don't care for its resources. It's humans who may not survive if we aren't wise about how we use our planet and all the good it has to offer.

Don't Hate... Participate!

There are many ways that you can help keep our world rich with resources.

- Use renewable resources such as solar power to charge your favorite gadgets.
- Reuse something old and make something new from it.
- Turn off water and lights when they're not in use.
- Walk or ride your bike to school.
- Drink from reusable water bottles.
- Take a shower, not a bath. You can save tons of water this way!

Limits to Growth

In her bestselling book, *Limits to Growth*, author Donella Meadows writes, "We cannot have infinite growth on a finite planet. Earth's supplies...will not be able to continuously satisfy the needs of a rapidly expanding global population and its increasing material demands."

Mother Earth gives us everything we need to survive. But if we continue to take, take, take and never give back...eventually, we will run out.

Think Like a Scientist

What are the effects of overexploitation? Experiment and find out!

What to Get

- bowls
- popped popcorn

What to Do

1. Gather a big group of family or friends. Give everyone a bowl.

2. Give each person a number from 1 to however many people you are, such as 1 to 10.

3. Have the person with the number 1 fill his or her bowl with as much popcorn as he or she pleases.

4. Have the person with the number 2 do the same. Keep going one at a time until the last person has had a turn.

5. What happened? Did everyone get popcorn? Were the amounts even? Think of each person as a "generation." Did anyone think about the next generations when getting his or her popcorn? What might have been done differently?

Glossary

aquifer—underground beds of rock or soil that contain or transmit water

biological—of or related to living things

chemicals—substances made when atoms or molecules change

complex—not easy to understand or explain

depleted—reduced or used up

extraction—the act or process of removing something

fossil fuels—fuels that are formed in Earth from dead plants or animals

industries—businesses

natural resources—things existing in the natural world, such as wood, oil, or minerals

overexploitation—use of a resource to the point of severe depletion, collapse, and even destruction

radioactive—giving off energy as a substance's atomic nuclei break apart

renewable—able to be replenished

scarce—limited

Index

From Resource to You

Look around and take notice of five different things you have used today. Write them in a list. Next to each one, write what it's made of. Water? Wood? Plastic? Metal? All of the above? Now, write where you think the materials came from and the resources that were used to make them. What do you think it took to get those things from the original resource to you?